Extravagant GENEROSITY

The Heart of Giving

MICHAEL REEVES & JENNIFER TYLER

Small-Group Leader Guide
Sally D. Sharpe

ABINGDON PRESS
Nashville, Tennessee

EXTRAVAGANT GENEROSITY:
THE HEART OF GIVING
Small-Group Leader Guide

Copyright © 2011 Abingdon Press

This book is printed on acid-free paper.

Extravagant generosity : the heart of giving, Michael Reeves and Jennifer Tyler : leader guide / by Sally D. Sharpe.
    p. cm.
 ISBN 978-1-4267-2911-9 (trade pbk. : alk. paper)
 1. Christian giving--Study and teaching. 2. Generosity--Religious aspects--Christianity--Study and teaching. 3. Christian giving--United Methodist Church (U.S.) I. Reeves, Michael, Dr. Extravagant generosity. II. Title.
 BV772.S475 2011
 248'.6071--dc22

                                     2011008809

11 12 13 14 15 16 17 18 19 20--10 9 8 7 6 5 4 3 2
MANUFACTURED IN THE UNITED STATES OF AMERICA

Extravagant Generosity: The Heart of Giving

Small-Group Leader Guide

CONTENTS

INTRODUCTION

Based on the fifth principle in Bishop Robert Schnase's groundbreaking book *Five Practices of Fruitful Congregations, Extravagant Generosity* is a unique stewardship program designed to help your church both teach and practice a biblical way of giving that focuses on the abundance of God's grace and the Christian's need to give, rather than on the church's need for money. Through this comprehensive program, your congregation will be encouraged to give, share, sacrifice, and serve extravagantly and joyfully out of love for God and neighbor. This new model of giving will result in positive and dramatic change—not only in the lives of those touched by your generosity, but also in the lives of individuals and families within your church.

This leader's guide is designed to help you facilitate a small group experience during the four weeks of the Extravagant Generosity emphasis in your church. Throughout these four weeks, everyone in the congregation is invited to join in reading brief daily devotions from *Practicing Extravagant Generosity: Daily Readings on the Grace of Giving,* by Robert Schnase. Once a week—whether on Sunday morning, Wednesday evening, or some other time of your choosing—your small group will meet together to reflect on the readings for the week and to share insights and ideas related to your own faith journeys and your congregation's ministry.

Each session outline, which can be adapted for either a 45- or 60-minute group session, includes the following elements:

The Message
This one-sentence summary of the main theme gives you the "big picture" for the group session. Read this for your own information or feel free to share with the group, if you like.

Scripture / Opening Prayer (5 minutes)
This segment provides a concise biblical foundation for the session in three segments: reading the Scripture, reflecting on the Scripture, and responding to the Scripture through prayer.

Video (3 minutes)

A short video that includes words and phrases, images, music, and sound effects serves as bridge from the Scripture to the other components of the session—Points to Ponder, Group Discussion, and Group Activity—setting the tone and mood for the session.

Points to Ponder (10 minutes)

This section highlights themes and excerpts from the weekly devotions in *Practicing Extravagant Generosity: Daily Readings on the Grace of Giving* by Robert Schnase. Choose 2-3 from those provided to share and discuss, customizing the session to the interests and sensibilities of your particular group.

Group Discussion (15-20 minutes)

A dozen or more questions are provided to generate discussion on the various themes and points highlighted in the session. More are provided than you will have time for; put a checkmark beside those you wish to discuss in your group.

Group Activity (10-15 minutes)

First, participants are invited to share their responses to the question that was included on the card mailed to the congregation during the week. Then a simple activity allows them to respond or take some form of action.

Closing Prayer (2-5 minutes)

A short prayer is provided, or you may choose to offer your own prayer. Time is also allowed for sharing prayer concerns and customizing your prayer time as the group desires.

Making It Your Own

The key to a successful group experience is to make it your own. Feel free to adapt, modify, or expand the material provided for each session as you wish to meet the specific needs of your group. Here are some ideas you might consider.

- Add your own Points to Ponder. Scan the devotions in *Practicing Extravagant Generosity: Daily Readings on the Grace of Giving,* marking your favorite passages with a highlighter. Share these with the group during the Points to Ponder segment.

- Modify the group activity to meet the specific interests or particular makeup of your group. No one knows your group better than you do.

- Create your own opening and closing prayers, or invite a different person to pray each time.

- If your group enjoys singing, add a song either at the start or close of each session. Try to choose a song that relates to the week's theme.

- Set aside a couple of minutes at the end of each session for group members to share one "take away" they got from the lesson—something that really spoke to them or made an impact on them, or something they want to apply in their lives in the coming week.

- Take up a collection/offering each week and designate the money for a particular project or ministry important to your group.

- Create one or more follow-up activities that your group can do outside of class time—or after the four-week emphasis has ended—to reinforce application of principles and ideas you have discussed as well as contribute to or extend the church-wide focus.

- Rotate and/or share leadership. Invite a different person to facilitate the group session each week. Or, share responsibilities for facilitating each session among various group members, inviting one person to read the Scripture, one to share reflections on the Scripture, one to pray, one to facilitate group discussion, and one to lead the group activity. Use the same individuals each week, or invite different people to participate week to week. Be sure to give them advance notice.

Preparing to Lead

However you choose to customize the group sessions, here are a few helpful hints to keep in mind as you prepare to lead your group. (Note: If you plan to invite one or more persons to help facilitate group discussion, be sure to share these tips with those individuals as well.)

- Read the week's devotional readings in *Practicing Extravagant Generosity* and review the session outline prior to the group session.

- Determine whether you will focus on the suggested Points to Ponder (drawn from the week's devotional readings) or substitute others. Remember that you will need to create your own discussion questions for any additional points.

- Communicate the benefit of honest and open conversation—for them as individuals and as a group. Encourage individuals to share from their own life experiences as they are willing.

- If no one responds at first, do not be afraid of a little silence. Count to seven silently; then say something such as, "Would anyone like to go first?" If everyone remains silent, venture a response yourself. Then ask for comments and other responses.

- Model openness as you share with the group. Group members will follow your example. If you share at a surface level, everyone else will follow suit.

- Draw out participants without asking them to share what they are unwilling to share. Make eye contact with someone and say something such as, "How about someone else?"

- Encourage multiple responses before moving on.

- Ask "Why?" or "Why do you believe that?" to help continue a discussion and give it greater depth.

- Affirm others' responses with comments such as, "Great" or "Thanks" or "Good insight"—especially if this is the first time someone has spoken during the session.

- Give everyone a chance to talk, but keep the conversation moving. Moderate to prevent a few individuals from doing all the talking.

- Monitor your own contributions. If you are doing most of the talking, back off so that you do not train the group not to respond.

- Remember that you do not have to have all the "answers." Your job is to keep the discussion going and encourage participation.

- Honor the time schedule. If a session is running longer than expected, get consensus from the group before continuing beyond the agreed-upon ending time.

- Pray—for your group members individually and for God's presence and leading before each session.

Above all else, prayer is the most important thing you will do in preparation for this group experience. Prayer will both encourage and empower you in every aspect of leading your group. In the weeks ahead, may your group come to a deeper understanding and appreciation of what it means to practice Extravagant Generosity.

A QUICK OVERVIEW OF
THE CHURCH-WIDE PROGRAM

Extravagant Generosity: The Heart of Giving is a theologically sound, creative stewardship approach that is simple in design and built around functions that are easy to understand and implement. The objective of this program is, over time, to change the culture in your church from fundraising to generosity as a core value of discipleship. The effective methods and procedures can be used year after year to ultimately cultivate an environment of generosity. This program features tools for adults, youth, and children. Recognizing churches vary in technical ability, resources provided are adaptable, based on capability.

Program Steps

The program is planned and carried out in five steps, described in the Program Guide:

Step 1. Decide

Step 2. Assemble

Step 3. Prepare

Step 4. Execute

Step 5. Implement

These steps, begun by the pastor or church leadership, are carried out by a program director and program teams, and ultimately by all church members. When the planning is over and the groundwork has been laid, the program is implemented with the congregation over the course of four weeks, with four Sundays of special focus, including worship, sermons, and Sunday school or small-group activities. The fourth Sunday is Response Sunday, or Commitment Sunday.

In planning your schedule, allow five weeks for preparation, then another four weeks for the program itself. A good way to do this is to pick a date for Response Sunday, then count back four weeks plus five weeks. That will determine the start date for Step 1.

Program Components

Practicing Extravagant Generosity: Daily Readings on the Grace of Giving
A devotional guide written by Bishop Robert Schnase, designed to help everyone in your congregation understand and experience God's call to a life of Extravagant Generosity.

Program Guide with CD-ROM
An overview of the program's concepts, functions, and activities. The CD-ROM provides all the tools and materials you need to implement the program.

Timeline
A quick overview that reflects the steps, functions, and pulse of the program. It also serves as an orientation and ongoing guide for team leaders.

Small-Group Leader Guide
Brief instructions and suggestions for those facilitating the small-group study.

Small-Group and Worship DVD
Videos to help participants explore and encounter the grace of giving, to be used in worship and small-group settings.

Planning Kit
Contains all of the items listed above, conveniently packaged together.

WEEK 1

EKG: Ministry Flows from the Heart
Lesson Time: 45-60 minutes

The Message
Sharing and good deeds result in vibrant, healthy life—in our personal lives and in our church.

Scripture / Prayer (5 minutes)

Reading the Scripture
Invite one or more participants to read aloud the following Scriptures. (If you like, write the passages on a board or chart in advance.)

> *Command those who are rich in this present world not to be arrogant nor to put their hope in wealth, which is so uncertain, but to put their hope in God, who richly provides us with everything for our enjoyment. Command them to do good, to be rich in good deeds, and to be generous and willing to share. In this way they will lay up treasure for themselves as a firm foundation for the coming age, so that they may take hold of the life that is truly life. (1 Timothy 6:17-19 NIV)*

> *For where your treasure is, there your heart will be also. (Matthew 6:21 NRSV)*

Reflecting on the Scripture
Read aloud the following commentary adapted from the sermon outline material provided on the Resource CD-ROM, or be prepared to paraphrase it in your own words:

> *We are materially blessed in our country when compared to the rest of the world's population. Though some of us may have made choices that do not leave very much margin financially, the fact is that, by most standards, we are well off. Often it seems that the more we have, the more we worry about keeping what we have and getting*

more. When that is the focus of our thoughts, expressing faith in God becomes more of a challenge.

Paul's remedy expressed in 1 Timothy 6:17-19 is to put our faith in God, and he enumerates several ways to do that. He suggests that we do good, that we be rich in good deeds, and that we be generous and willing to share. Then he says there is a difference between merely living in our culture and intentionally living a Christian life, which he calls "truly life."

Responding to the Scripture

Pray aloud:
Lord, thank you for speaking to us through your word. Give us wisdom, understanding, and insight as we reflect and share together so that we may discern how you are calling us to respond. Amen.

Video (3 minutes)

This short video serves as a bridge from the Scripture you've just explored to the remainder of the group session. Consisting of words and phrases, images, music, and sound effects, it sets a tone and mood for all that is to follow, preparing participants to engage in discussion and application of the key points and themes included in this week's session. Dim the lights and play the video for Week 1, "EKG: Ministry Flows from the Heart."

Points to Ponder (10 minutes)

Choose 2-3 of the following points drawn from the devotions in *Practicing Extravagant Generosity: Daily Readings on the Grace of Giving* by Robert Schnase. Summarize or present each in your own words, reading aloud excerpts as you choose (printed in bold). You might find it beneficial to include the point from the devotion highlighted in this week's sermon outline, which is marked with an asterisk. Ask participants to hold all questions and comments for group discussion time, which will follow.

Week 1, Monday

Generosity is an aspect of character; it flows from the heart.

We don't hear much about stewardship outside the church. It's a term that is not easily understood by those new to the church. But we all know what generosity is. It is an aspect of character that we recognize in others and long to have ourselves. Its opposite is selfishness, self-centeredness, and greed. Schnase writes, **"No stories from Scripture tell of people living the God-related spiritual life while fostering a greedy attitude. Generosity extends beyond merely the use of money, although it most definitely includes that. There are generous spirits; generous souls; people who are generous with their time, with their teaching, with their love. Generosity finds many biblical sources, and is a fruit of the Spirit (Galatians 5:22-23)." (p. 12)** Generosity flows from the heart—first from God's heart into ours, and then from our hearts into the world.

Week 1, Tuesday

Generosity is always for the benefit of others; it is selfless, not self-serving.*

The author recalls one spring when he saw various birds preparing to build their nests. He notes that the activity of building nests is often used as a metaphor to describe people providing for their own comfort or security. He then points out that the nests built by birds are not for the birds who build them; they are for their young, the next generation. Like birds, we build "nests" in our churches—such as buildings, programs, ministries, jobs, and various services. We need to ask ourselves if these nests are for our own comfort or for the benefit of future generations. Schnase asks, **"Does our giving serve us and our needs or serve God by serving the mission of the church to reach new people?" (p. 15)** If we want to be a healthy congregation, we must focus on those who are outside the congregation as much as we do on those who are inside.

Week 1, Wednesday

Extravagant generosity has "wings"; it makes a difference beyond our sight and our time.

After reflecting on the helicopter-like seeds he noticed one day while hiking with his sons, Schnase recounts the parable of the sower and comments that the "seeds with wings," as his son called them, add a new dimension to the parable. He acknowledges that so much of our impact affects those closest to us, which is our calling. But he notes that we have a larger calling as well, which is to give our seeds wings so that the good we do and the difference we make extend beyond our sight and our time. In conclusion he writes, **"There** is no end to what God can accomplish anywhere in the world when our 'seeds have wings'; when we are willing to let our prayers, intentions, plans, efforts, and work be lifted by the Spirit to places far away. . . ." (p. 19)

Week 1, Thursday

Generosity helps us achieve God's purposes in ourselves.

The author recalls a couple who, after deciding to partner with God to help their church reach more people by building a new sanctuary, gave the largest gift they had ever given. The gift became one of the great delights of their lives, assuring them that they could make a difference. Schnase notes that we give so that we can achieve God's purposes in ourselves. In other words, God uses our giving to change us and give us different motivations. He writes, "**Giving moderates the powerful and sometimes destructively insatiable drive for acquisition. In the daily interior struggle fostered by a consumerist, materialist society that pressures us to pursue many things that do not lead to real happiness, the practice of giving aims us at what ultimately satisfies. Giving . . . constantly resets the internal compass in the right direction. Generosity becomes a tool God uses to draw us closer to God and to align us more closely with God's desire for us." (p. 21)**

Week 1, Friday

When we practice generosity regularly, we develop the "muscle memory" for giving; it becomes part of who we are.

In telling about Sarah, who has practiced tithing since she was a little girl, Schnase includes this quote from Sarah: "**Tithing was learned and practiced so early that I developed the muscle memory for giving. Like practicing my tennis serve for so many years that I don't have to think about each step, my giving is part of who I am." (p. 22)** He suggests that with practice, anyone can develop this kind of muscle memory. Tithing, he says, reminds us that our ultimate worth comes from the assurance that we are children of God and are infinitely loved by God. It gives us new and improved perspective so that we are able to see the "traps, deceptions, and myths" of our consumerist society. As a result, we are strengthened and equipped to serve God's purposes.

Week 1, Saturday

Giving changes the giver, the recipient, and the congregation.

In this devotion the author gives the example of a group that was studying *Five Practices of Fruitful Congregations*. Each week the leader asked the participants to empty the spare change in their pockets, purses, and wallets into a plastic bowl. In the last session, as they talked about Extravagant Generosity, she revealed that the $300 in change they had collected would be donated to the Nothing But Nets compaign, which saves lives in Africa by providing medicated mosquito nets to prevent people from getting malaria. Schanse observes that this simple and painless exercise done during a group study will save children's lives on the other side of the world. He writes, **"Even pocket change changes lives. Change the life of a child and you change the world." (p. 25)**

Week 1, Sunday

Churches that practice Extravagant Generosity emphasize the Christian's need to give more than the church's need for money.

In this devotion, the author highlights the attitudes and habits of churches that practice Extravagant Generosity. Based on his observations, we can create two lists of do's and don'ts for congregations seeking to grow in generosity:

DO

1. Speak confidently and faithfully about money, giving, generosity, and the difference giving makes for the purposes of Christ in the world and in the life of the giver.
2. Emphasize the Christian's need to give.
3. Teach, preach, and practice proportional giving with the goal of tithing.
4. Use God's name accurately by appealing to the highest of life-giving purposes for giving.
5. Speak of joy, devotion, honoring God, and the steady growth of spirit that leads to greater generosity.

DON'T

1. Talk in general terms about stewardship.
2. Emphasize the church's need for money.
3. Treat proportional giving and tithing as if they are optional and unessential.
4. Employ fear, guilt, pressure, and shame as motivation for giving.
5. Apologize, groan, whine, act embarrassed, or feel awkward as you encourage giving.
6. Treat giving as if it is a duty or an obligation.
7. Hold pledge campaigns that are about money, dollars, and budgets.
8. Allow stewardship efforts to focus on

DO

6. Delight in giving.
7. Hold pledge campaigns that are about mission, spiritual growth, and relationship to God.
8. See that stewardship efforts deepen prayer life, build community, unite people with purpose, and clarify mission.
9. Express gratitude to serve God through giving.
10. Encourage people to grow in their giving
11. Share stories of lives changed by practicing generosity.
12. Publically thank God for the generosity of the people.
13. Express personal appreciation to those who give.
14. Cultivate the hearts of the people in the way of Christ.
15. Emphasize mission, purpose, and life-changing results.
16. Provide a compelling vision that invites joyous giving resulting in meaning and purpose.

DON'T

the church as an institution, rather than its people and purpose.
9. Be reluctant or resentful when it comes to serving God through giving.
10. Allow people to stagnate in their giving.
11. Keep stories of generosity secret for fear of embarrassing or offending anyone.
12. Forget to publically thank God for the generosity of the people.
13. Take for granted those who give.
14. Neglect the hearts of the people in the way of Christ.
15. Emphasize shortages, budgets, and institutional loyalty.
16. Coast along without a vision that spurs members to find meaning and purpose through giving.

Schnase concludes, **"[Churches that practice Extravagant Generosity] know that God moves people to give in order to find purpose and to accomplish things for Christ. They connect money with mission. They give offerings of whatever they can, whenever they can—they excel in the grace of giving." (p. 27)**

Group Discussion (15-20 minutes)
Select from the following:

1. How would you explain the difference between stewardship and generosity? Which most helpfully inspires your giving as you seek to grow in the image of God and in service to Christ?
2. What motivates you to give? What motivates you to support specific ministries of your congregation?
3. How does your giving shape or affect your relationship to God?

4. How has giving changed you?
5. Name some of the "nests" that your church is devoting time, energy, and resources to build (e.g., buildings, programs, ministries, jobs, services). Which of these nests are for the comfort or benefit of those inside the church? Which serve the mission of the church to reach new people?
6. What does it mean to give your generosity "wings"? How is this possible?
7. How has your personal generosity affected the lives of those beyond your own home?
8. How has your church's generosity affected the lives of those beyond your church walls? In other words, how does your church practice generosity to reach the community—and beyond? How do you support and participate in the mission of your church?
9. Do you believe that tithing (giving 10% of income) is an appropriate giving goal for Christians? Why or why not?
10. In what way does the regular practice of tithing (or proportional giving) develop "muscle memory" for giving?
11. If you practice tithing, what benefits have you experienced from it?
12. Have you ever given over and beyond your normal tithe or pattern of giving? If so, what was the experience like?
13. Do you find that the more you give, the more likely you are to give? Why or why not?
14. What results when we are willing to share and do good? What has been the greatest benefit of your giving?

Group Activity (10-15 minutes)

Invite participants to respond briefly to the following question. If you like, write their answers on a board or chart.

What do you love most about our church?

Pause and give thanks for these evidences of God's presence and love demonstrated through individuals, groups, and ministries of your church. Have one person pray, or allow group members to offer thanks spontaneously.

Brainstorm ways that these strengths or assets of your church might be utilized or built upon to reach/serve those . . .
1) beyond your church to the community
2) beyond your local area

Closing Prayer (2-5 minutes)

End with a time of prayer. You may use the prayer provided, offer your own prayer, invite someone from the group to pray (ask in advance, if possible), or allow participants to pray as they are led. If your group has a practice of sharing prayer concerns, do that first and pray for those requests as well.

Generous God, you are the giver of all good things. You have created us in your image and called us to be generous and to do good. Help us to release our hold on all that you have given us, acknowledging that all we have and all we are belongs to you. Remind us that striving after worldly possessions and selfish pursuits is hollow and empty and that the practice of giving actually directs us toward what ultimately satisfies. May our giving draw us closer to you and align us with your desires for us. Amen.

WEEK 2

The Art of Love: Relationships Are Matters of the Heart
Lesson Time: 45-60 minutes

The Message
Our relationships with one another prove we know and love God.

Scripture / Opening Prayer (5 minutes)

Reading the Scripture
Invite one or more participants to read aloud the following Scriptures. (If you like, write the passages on a board or chart in advance.)

> *Hear therefore, O Israel, and observe them diligently, so that it may go well with you, and so that you may multiply greatly in a land flowing with milk and honey, as the LORD, the God of your ancestors, has promised you. Hear, O Israel: The LORD is our God, the LORD alone. You shall love the LORD your God with all your heart, and with all your soul, and with all your might. Keep these words that I am commanding you today in your heart. (Deuteronomy 6:3-6 NRSV)*

> *I give you a new commandment, that you love one another. Just as I have loved you, you also should love one another. By this everyone will know that you are my disciples, if you have love for one another." (John 13:34-35 NRSV)*

Reflecting on the Scripture
Read aloud the following commentary adapted from the sermon outline material provided on the Resource CD-ROM, or be prepared to paraphrase it in your own words:

> *In this passage from Deuteronomy, we find the great Shema, that proclamation of spiritual focus and priority that is a basic teaching of our faith. Any picture of the Wailing Wall in Jerusalem will show Orthodox Jews rocking back and forth while reciting the Shema.*

> *In the Christian faith, we give attention to the Shema in the context of the teaching of Jesus found in John 13:34-35. There is a clear expectation that one of the ways we express our love for God is by loving one another. Sometimes this can be difficult for us.*

Responding to the Scripture

Pray aloud:
Lord, thank you for speaking to us through your word. Give us wisdom, understanding, and insight as we reflect and share together so that we may discern how you are calling us to respond. Amen.

Video (3 minutes)

This short video serves as a bridge from the Scripture you've just explored to the remainder of the group session. Consisting of words and phrases, images, music, and sound effects, it sets a tone and mood for all that is to follow, preparing participants to engage in discussion and application of the key points and themes included in this week's session. Dim the lights and play the video for Week 2, "The Art of Love: Relationships Are Matters of the Heart."

Points to Ponder (10 minutes)

Choose 2-3 of the following points drawn from the devotions in *Practicing Extravagant Generosity: Daily Readings on the Grace of Giving* by Robert Schnase. Summarize or present each in your own words, reading aloud excerpts as you choose (printed in bold). You might find it beneficial to include the point from the devotion highlighted in this week's sermon outline, which is marked with an asterisk. Ask participants to hold all questions and comments for group discussion time, which will follow.

Week 2, Monday

Through our giving, God changes lives, and in changing them, transforms us.

The author recounts the story of the fiddle player in the movie *Cold Mountain* who discovers real joy and meaning in playing the fiddle after being challenged by a dying girl to go beyond his limited repertoire and make up a song for her. He notes that when the fiddle player discovered how to use that ordinary fiddle and the simple gift of music for higher purposes, it became sacred. And when he discovered the gift he had been given and the power of that gift to bring good in the world, he was changed.

Schnase writes, **"We find something similar through the practice of Extravagant Generosity. Giving causes life. Before, our giving may have been arbitrary, perfunctory, haphazard, a little here and there. But when we discover the great difference generosity makes; place it in service to God; and use our resources to relieve suffering, strengthen communities, and restore relationships, then we look at giving entirely differently. . . .We want to improve our generosity at every turn until it becomes as easy as drawing breath."** (pp. 32-33)

Week 2, Tuesday

We must keep learning, growing, changing, and adapting if we are to embrace God's will for us and navigate through this rapidly changing world.

The author recalls a harrowing rafting trip with his sons down the Pacuare River in Costa Rica. The rapids were fierce and constant, and the guide told them that the only way they could have any control over the direction they were going was to move a little faster than the current below them. That meant they had to paddle constantly so they would not be pushed along out of control. Schanse notes, **"If we want to navigate with purpose and to control our direction rather than becoming a victim to forces beyond our control, we have to keep paddling."** (p. 35)

Observing that we live "fast-forward lives" in a rapidly changing world, the author acknowledges that we often feel like victims—powerless and vulnerable. He encourages us to keep paddling—keep learning, growing, changing, adapting, and giving our best. The key to remaining strong, he suggests, is rethinking things, praying each day, constantly recommitting to the right things, and repeatedly practicing the disciplines that keep us connected to God. He concludes, **"Life requires an agility of spirit, forward movement, effort, vision, and a keen awareness of the forces at work around us and how to use them for the purposes of Christ rather than become overwhelmed by them."** (p. 36)

Week 2, Wednesday

When we know and love God, we naturally respond to the needs of others with loving generosity.

In this reading the author tells the story of a part-time custodian at a downtown congregation who was taking out the trash when he saw a homeless man in the alley beside the church. He put down the garbage, pulled out his wallet, and gave the man a few dollars along with some kind words. The pastor, who was leaving the church at the time and saw what happened, was surprised and humbled by the custodian's unsolicited generosity. In contrast to the custodian's spontaneous generosity, the staff had spent hours trying to come up with policies and procedures for relating to the homeless population.

Schnase writes, **"The pastor asked the custodian why he gave the money and pressed him about whether he thought the homeless person might misuse the money for alcohol or drugs. 'I always do what I can,' the janitor answered. 'I give them a little money and say, God bless you, because I figure that they are some mother's son, some father's child, and so I give them something. What they do with the money—well, they have to answer to God about that. I have to answer to God about what I do with mine.'"** (p. 38)

Week 2, Thursday

Giving is returning to God what belongs to God already.

The author describes two attitudes toward possessions: 1) We consider all we have—our money, house, property—as owned by God and belonging to God, or 2) We believe our material possessions belong to us and, therefore, we can do with them as we please. He notes that when we have the first attitude, we are grateful for the privilege of managing God's resources for God's purposes and returning to God what already belongs to God. We desire to spend our money wisely and responsibly, not frivolously, and to invest it in ways that do not dishonor God's purposes. When we have the second attitude, on the other hand, he says that we do whatever we please with what we own and feel that God should be grateful for our generosity.

Schnase asks, **"Which perspective is truer, more ethically sound, more aligned with reality? . . . Which perspective fosters better decisions and deepens a spiritually grounded sense of community and responsibility? The wisdom revealed in Scripture and tradition for more than three thousand years is that those who practice from the perspective of a steward find greater happiness."** (p. 40)

Week 2, Friday

Just as we have freely received, so we are to freely give.*

In this devotion, the author points out that it is through giving of ourselves as God has given to us that we help the body of Christ flourish. He writes, **"Every sanctuary and chapel in which we have worshiped, every church** organ that has lifted our spirits, every pew where we have sat, every Communion rail where we have knelt, every hymnal from which we have sung, every praise band that has touched our hearts, every church classroom where we have gathered with our friends, every church kitchen that has prepared our meals, every church van that has taken us to camp, every church camp cabin where we have slept—all are the fruit of someone's Extravagant Generosity." (p. 41)

Week 2, Saturday

To paraphrase John Wesley, generosity is doing good in all the ways you can to all the people you can for as long as you can.

The author recalls this famous saying of John Wesley:

**Do all the good you can,
By all the means you can,
In all the ways you can,
In all the places you can,
At all the times you can,
To all the people you can,
As long as ever you can.**

He notes that, for Wesley, all things belong to God and are to be used to deepen our relationship with God and positively impact the world for God's purposes. This kind of mindset changes the way we earn, save, spend, and give money. In conclusion he writes, **"No stories from Scripture tell of people living the God-related spiritual life while fostering a greedy, self-centered, self-serving attitude. Knowing God leads to generosity."** (p. 44)

Week 2, Sunday

Giving adjusts our priorities and protects us from greed.

The author comments that, when asked how much money they would need to earn to be happy, people generally say they would be satisfied if they earned just 20 percent more than their current income. He notes that this attitude is a prescription for perpetual discontent, because you are always pursuing a receding goal.

Schnase observes that accepting the culture's myths about money and desirable lifestyles only perpetuates discontent. He writes, **"Forty-year-olds feel like failures because they are not millionaires; families buy houses beyond their capacity to afford; people pine for what they cannot possess. We wallow in abundance while suffering from a self-proclaimed scarcity. Despite the fact that we live in better houses, earn more money, drive nicer cars, spend more on entertainment, and enjoy greater conveniences than ninety percent of the world's population, or than we ourselves enjoyed thirty years ago, we never have enough." (p. 46)**

Extravagant giving is a way of putting God first and getting our priorities in order. It makes a statement about what we value and makes money our servant rather than our master. The author concludes, **"Giving provides a spiritually healthy detachment from the most harmful influences of a materialist society, an emotional distance that is otherwise unattainable. Giving protects us from the pangs of greed." (pp. 46-47)**

Group Discussion (15-20 minutes)
Select from the following:

1. What is the best or most joyful experience you have had in giving?
2. When was a time you felt that God transformed your life because you gave?
3. In what ways can you improve your generosity?
4. Have you ever witnessed an unexpected and extraordinary act of generosity? What happened?
5. How has another person's generosity influenced your own practice of giving?
6. Who is learning from your examples of generosity? How are you teaching others—such as children or grandchildren—to practice generosity?
7. Which view do you hold, that all we own belongs to God and we should manage these resources for God's purposes, or that our possessions belong to us and we can do with them as we like? How does this belief shape your actions? Your giving?
8. How have you been the recipient of another person's Extravagant Generosity? What was your reaction and why?
9. Have you ever been the recipient of a congregation's Extravagant Generosity? What was your reaction and why?
10. How have you been the recipient of God's Extravagant Generosity? How have you responded and why?
11. How do generosity and giving change the values that guide your earning, saving, and spending habits?

12. How does your relationship to God affect how you earn and budget your money (how you invest it, spend it, and share it with others)?
13. Have you ever changed how you earn or budget (invent, spend, share) your money because of your desire to follow Christ more closely?
14. How does your family talk about money and what makes for true happiness?

Group Activity (10-15 minutes)
Invite participants to respond briefly to the following question. If you like, write their answers on a board or chart.

Who in our church family has made a difference in your spiritual life?

Pause and give thanks for all of these people who have influenced your lives by extending Christ's grace and lovingkindness through generous acts of service, instruction, assistance, sacrifice, encouragement, and love. Have one person pray, or allow group members to offer thanks spontaneously.

Discuss specific ways you may "pay it forward" and continue the legacy of giving. List these on a board or chart if you like. Challenge participants to consider how God may be spurring them on to grow in the ways they give and serve.

Closing Prayer (2-5 minutes)
End with a time of prayer. You may use the prayer provided, offer your own prayer, invite someone from the group to pray (ask in advance, if possible), or allow participants to pray as they are led. If your group has a practice of sharing prayer concerns, do that first and pray for those requests as well.

> *Gracious God, knowing you is the key to Extravagant Generosity. The more we know you and experience your extravagant love for us, the more we want to bless others by generously giving of ourselves and our resources. And as we do, we not only change the lives of others; our own lives are transformed. Show us how we can improve our generosity more and more, so that eventually it becomes as easy and natural as breathing. We ask you to multiply our giving, Lord, so that it touches those who benefit directly from it and those who are only witnesses. Amen.*

Bucket Lists: Vision and Hope Are Inspirations of the Heart
Lesson Time: 45-60 minutes

The Message
God-sized vision requires faith and stepping out of your comfort zone.

Scripture / Opening Prayer (5 minutes)

Reading the Scripture
Invite one or more participants to read aloud the following Scriptures. (If you like, write the passages on a board or chart in advance.)

> *"Then afterward I will pour out my spirit on all flesh; your sons and your daughters shall prophesy, your old men shall dream dreams, and your young men shall see visions." (Joel 2:28 NRSV)*

> *So if you have been raised with Christ, seek the things that are above, where Christ is, seated at the right hand of God. (Colossians 3:1 NRSV)*

> *"But strive first for the kingdom of God and his righteousness, and all these things will be given to you as well." (Matthew 6:33 NRSV)*

Reflecting on the Scripture
Read aloud the following commentary adapted from the sermon outline material provided on the Resource CD-ROM, or be prepared to paraphrase it in your own words:

> *Today we are considering the issue of the vision of the church. Joel 2:28 offers some directions for us. Vision comes about as God inspires people to prophesy, dream, and have visions. Think silently for a moment about what God has inspired you to envision for the coming year.*

> *Then in Colossians 3:1 we are instructed to set our hearts on things above. Too often we are so overwhelmed by the dominant cultural influences in our life that it is very difficult to think in this way.*
>
> *Finally, in Matthew 6:33 our personal priorities are identified. As children of God, we should first seek to find our place in the Kingdom of God and strive for righteousness or right standing with God.*
>
> *These verses give us the starting place for understanding what God has called us to do and be as a church in the coming year.*

Responding to the Scripture

Pray aloud:

> *Lord, thank you for speaking to us through your word. Give us wisdom, understanding, and insight as we reflect and share together so that we may discern how you are calling us to respond. Amen.*

Video (3 minutes)

This short video serves as a bridge from the Scripture you've just explored to the remainder of the group session. Consisting of words and phrases, images, music, and sound effects, it sets a tone and mood for all that is to follow, preparing participants to engage in discussion and application of the key points and themes included in this week's session. Dim the lights and play the video for Week 3, "Bucket Lists: Vision and Hope Are Inspirations of the Heart."

Points to Ponder (10 minutes)

Choose 2-3 of the following points drawn from the devotions in *Practicing Extravagant Generosity: Daily Readings on the Grace of Giving* by Robert Schnase. Summarize or present each in your own words, reading aloud excerpts as you choose (printed in bold). You might find it beneficial to include the point from the devotion highlighted in this week's sermon outline, which is marked with an asterisk. Ask participants to hold all questions and comments for group discussion time, which will follow.

Week 3, Monday

Giving changes us.

The author gives several biblical examples of generosity, including the widow who gave all she had, Zacchaeus who was transformed by his giving, the

Samaritan who demonstrated compassion, and God's self-giving in Christ. He says that these examples illustrate that extravagant giving is always joyfully life-changing. Schnase writes, **"God uses our practice of giving to reconfigure our interior life. By giving, we craft a different inner desire as the driving element of life. Our motivations change." (p. 52)**

Only by giving are we able to develop the inner qualities of generosity. The author states that generosity cannot be attained apart from the practice of giving; it is made evident only by our actions.

Week 3, Tuesday

Our giving makes a difference.

In this devotion, the author focuses on the ways we can make a difference through giving. He points out that some people give because they love their church and want the life-changing ministries of their congregation to prosper. They give so that others can receive what they themselves have received. He writes, **"The fruit of this giving is tangible and visible; it is both immediate and long-term. Churches with generous members offer more ministry, work with greater confidence, have less conflict, and make a greater impact on their communities and on the world." (p. 54)**

Another reason people give is because their contributions align with the purposes God wants them to fulfill in the world. The author suggests that when we sense God's call to make a difference—such as helping others, relieving suffering, teaching the spiritual life, or reaching young people—we can contribute our time or become personally involved in a ministry.

Still another way to make a difference is by supporting the ministry of others—contributing the resources that make possible the work we feel called to support. Schnase concludes, **"We please God by making the difference God wants us to make." (p. 54)**

Week 3, Wednesday

Giving helps us to maintain balance and perspective—to keep our priorities in line with God's priorities.

In this devotion, the author retells Tolstoy's short story "How Much Land Does a Man Need?" A man learns that if he will give the King all his money, he will have the opportunity to take possession of all the land he can encompass by walking around it in a single day. Because of his greed, he marks out more and more land until he realizes he must run back as fast as he can to reach the starting point before the sun sets. Exhausted from the run, he drops dead just within reach of the starting place.

The author reflects that we tend to be discontent with what we have, and that generosity helps us to maintain the balance and perspective we need to live in a healthy relationship with our possessions and the material world. He writes, **"Growing in the grace of giving is part of the Christian journey of faith, a response Christian disciples offer to God's call to make a difference in the world. Generosity enlarges the soul, realigns priorities, connects people to the body of Christ, and strengthens congregations to fulfill Christ's ministries."** (p. 57)

Week 3, Thursday

Changing our thinking about how we find contentment in life leads to generosity.*

Schnase tells of the apostle Paul's own battle with aligning his priorities with God's, which Paul describes in Philippians 4. The author says that generosity comes from a reorientation in our thinking about how we find contentment in life. He points out that the apostle Paul wrote, "I have learned to be content with whatever I have," yet Paul certainly did not lack initiative. On the contrary, Paul was industrious, competitive, and ambitious for God's kingdom work.

Schnase writes, **"Paul realized how seductive our activity and our appetite for more could become. We begin to believe that happiness depends upon outward circumstance and material comforts rather than deriving from inner spiritual qualities—love, peace, compassion, self-control, gentleness, prayerfulness. Possessing greater wealth does not mean that we experience contentedness. We can still feel panic, emptiness, striving, and isolation. We feel needy, and our appetites become insatiable. Surrounded by water, we are dying of thirst."** (p. 58)

So, how do we break the cycle of conditioned discontent? The author says it requires courageous soul work and requires generative relationships, mutual support, and knowing how to love and be loved. He writes, **"Contentment arises from seeking that which satisfies."** (p. 59)

Week 3, Friday

Giving makes following God real.

Schnase explores several Scriptures that remind us that greed obstructs our pathway to God and to the life God would have us enjoy. He points out that whereas unrestrained desire for material possessions leaves little room for God and causes us to abandon Jesus' mission, Extravagant Generosity enables us to live a God-related life. He concludes, **"The God-related life means our relationship with God influences all we do. When we seek to do the things God would have us do, including giving, our practice intensifies our love for the things God loves. Then the material possessions that can serve as a distraction or impediment to following Christ become an instrument for our serving Christ. Our material goods, consecrated to God, nourish our desire to serve God." (p. 62)**

Week 3, Saturday

Tithing is not only about what God wants us to do; it's also about who God wants us to become.

The author discusses how tithing is a concrete way to put God first and develop a Christ-like heart. He encourages us to pray honestly about our giving, asking what God would have us give up in order to tithe. He writes, **"The practice [of tithing] causes us to adapt our behaviors to someone else's will: God's. No one tithes accidentally. Extravagant Generosity requires focused soul work, deep conviction, a mature spirit, learning, practice, and extraordinary intentionality." (p. 64)** Schnase concludes by observing that tithing is more than a financial decision; it is a life decision that **"rearranges all the furniture of our interior lives" (p. 64),** resulting in spiritual blessing.

Week 3, Sunday

People who practice Extravagant Generosity change their lives in order to change the lives of others.

While reviewing the habits of those who practice Extravagant Generosity, Schnase points out that they
- give with joy—from the heart
- meet needs without being asked
- see situations through the eyes of faith, not fear
- persist in doing good
- pray, hope, and dream about the good they accomplish through their gifts
- consecrate their giving to God
- give without expecting anything in return

- are content with what they have
- avoid personal debt as much as possible
- save regularly
- avoid overindulgence and waste
- give thanks in all circumstances

He concludes with these words: **"People who practice Extravagant Generosity change lives. Their giving knows no bounds. They are rich toward God." (p. 66)**

Group Discussion (15-20 minutes)
Select from the following:

1. Do you sometimes feel that your life consists in the abundance of possessions? How does this make you feel?
2. How would you define greed? How can practicing generosity counteract greed and help balance the priorities of your life?
3. In terms of wealth and generosity, what does living a "God-related life" mean to you?
4. How is your life richer in the things that money cannot buy than it was a year ago?
5. Have you practiced the tithe, regularly offering ten percent of your income to God? If so, how has this practice affected your spiritual life? If not, what keeps you from doing so?
6. How would you define or explain Extravagant Generosity? How would you describe someone who practices this kind of giving?
7. What obstacles prevent you from practicing Extravagant Generosity? Which is the *greatest* obstacle to your generosity?
8. How does God use your giving to change you? How do you think practicing *greater* generosity would change you/your life?
9. How does your giving to God influence other aspects of your life?
10. How does God use your giving to make a difference—in your congregation and its ministries, in your community or region, and in the world?
11. When was a time you felt God's Spirit move you to increase your level of giving—to give resources beyond what you had previously given? What motivated you to make the gift? What resulted from the gift?
12. Why does Extravagant Giving require faith? Tell of a time when you stepped out of your comfort zone in faith to give generously.
13. How willing are you to make changes in the way you relate to money as you listen to God's voice in your life?

Group Activity (10-15 minutes)

Invite participants to respond briefly to the following questions. If you like, write their answers on a board or chart.

What is your vision and hope for your future? What is your vision and hope for our church?

Pause and pray about these dreams and hopes that have been expressed. Have one person pray, or allow group members to offer thanks spontaneously.

Consider one or two wide-reaching dreams that you can imagine tackling if people in your church worked together. Share ideas. Discuss: What steps can we take to pursue these dreams in the coming year?

Closing Prayer (2-5 minutes)

End with a time of prayer. You may use the prayer provided, offer your own prayer, invite someone from the group to pray (ask in advance, if possible), or allow participants to pray as they are led. If your group has a practice of sharing prayer concerns, do that first and pray for those requests as well.

> *God of vision and hope, you are the One who enables us to dream dreams. Today we ask you to help us set our minds on things above so that we might dream your dreams. Align our priorities with yours so that we desire to make changes in our lives—changes that will result in Extravagant Generosity. Replace our greed with contentment and our complacency about the needs of others with a passion to give and serve as Christ did. Move us out of our comfort zones, Lord, and fill us with faith so that we may practice greater generosity and grow in love—for you and for others. Amen.*

WEEK 4

Declarations of Your Heart
Lesson Time: 45-60 minutes

The Message
Our giving is an expression of what we love.

Scripture / Opening Prayer (5 minutes)

Reading the Scripture
Invite one or more participants to read aloud the following Scriptures. (If you like, write the passages on a board or chart in advance.)

> *"For God so loved the world that he gave his only Son, so that everyone who believes in him may not perish but may have eternal life." (John 3:16 NRSV)*

> *Therefore show these men the proof of your love and the reason for our pride in you, so that the churches can see it. (2 Corinthians 8:24 NIV)*

Reflecting on the Scripture
Read aloud the following commentary adapted from the sermon outline material provided on the Resource CD-ROM, or be prepared to paraphrase it in your own words:

> *The first few words of one of the most well-known Bible verses, John 3:16, clearly state that the way God showed his love for the world is by giving. Giving is part of the character of God according to Scripture. Robert Schnase puts it this way:*

> *We give because we are made in the image of God, whose essential nature is giving. We are created with God's nature imprinted on our souls; we are hard-wired to be social, compassionate, connected,*

*loving, and generous. God's extravagant generosity is part of our es-
sential nature as well. But we are anxious and fearful, influenced by
a culture that makes us believe we never have enough. God sent Jesus
Christ to bring us back to ourselves, and back to God. As we "have in
us the mind that was in Christ Jesus," we become free. (Practicing Extravagant Generosity, pp. 56-57)*

*In 2 Corinthians 8:24, the whole teaching is about giving, and the
apostle Paul concludes this thought by saying that our giving is a proof
of our love for God.*

Responding to the Scripture
Pray aloud:
> *Lord, thank you for speaking to us through your word. Give us
wisdom, understanding, and insight as we reflect and share together
so that we may discern how you are calling us to respond. Amen.*

Video (3 minutes)
This short video serves as a bridge from the Scripture you've just explored to
the remainder of the group session. Consisting of words and phrases, images,
music, and sound effects, it sets a tone and mood for all that is to follow, preparing participants to engage in discussion and application of the key points and
themes included in this week's session. Dim the lights and play the video for
Week 4, "Declarations of Your Heart."

Points to Ponder (10 minutes)
Choose 2-3 of the following points drawn from the devotions in *Practicing Extravagant Generosity: Daily Readings on the Grace of Giving* by Robert
Schnase. Summarize or present each in your own words, reading aloud excerpts
as you choose (printed in bold). You might find it beneficial to include the point
from the devotion highlighted in this week's sermon outline, which is marked
with an asterisk. Ask participants to hold all questions and comments for group
discussion time, which will follow.

Week 4, Monday

The condition of our hearts is revealed through our giving.*

Schnase observes, **"The people whom we admire and respect for their
generous spirits, spiritual wisdom, and deep-heartedness invariably have**

practiced giving in such an extravagant manner that it has reshaped them. God has used their long-term patterns of giving to form in them the spiritual qualities that cause them to be our mentors. They give extravagantly according to their means, and many beyond their means, and most practice or exceed the tithe." (p. 72)

When we love God and value the things that God values, we are eager to give our utmost and highest—even when it is challenging to do so. The author encourages us with these words: "Despite the outward challenges and inner struggles... where there is a desire to give, there is a way. The two coins dropped in the treasury from the hands of the poor widow... forever remind us that there is always a way. Giving helps us to become what God wants us to be." (p. 72)

Week 4, Tuesday

Giving generously is a discipline learned with time and practice.

The author acknowledges that the practice of tithing can be challenging to those new to the faith. He offers this advice: "Take it one step at a time and grow into it over a few years. If you are so overwhelmed with debt that you struggle under an oppressive anxiety, first make the changes in spending and lifestyle that grant you freedom from excessive debt. When you can breathe again, begin to give proportionally, and grow in the grace of giving toward the tithe." (p. 75)

He also encourages those who have been active in the church for years but do not tithe to think seriously and prayerfully about why they do not tithe. He asks, "Why are the other faith practices relevant and helpful, but the discipline of tithing is not? Is the avoidance of tithing a fruit of faithfulness, or the result of submission to the values of a consumerist culture?" (p. 75)

Week 4, Wednesday

Our giving (or lack of giving) reflects whether we are listening to the wisdom of the world or the wisdom of God.

In this reading, Schnase reflects on our materialistic and consumerist society. He notes that our culture encourages and feeds our desire for more, bigger, and better, perpetuating the idea that self-worth and happiness are found in owning material possessions. He writes, "Thirty-year-olds feel like failures because they don't already have the kind of house that their parents own.

Couples struggle under oppressive levels of debt that strain marriages, destroy happiness, and intensify conflict and anxiety. As one radio show host says, 'We buy things we don't even need with money we don't even have to impress people we don't even know!' (*The Dave Ramsey Show*)." (p. 78) The author points out that these are more than financial planning issues; they are spiritual problems. He challenges us to decide whether we will listen to the wisdom of the world or the wisdom of God.

Week 4, Thursday

If we want to become more generous, pruning is required.

Schanse unpacks the idea of pruning as it relates to growing in generosity. He suggests that it is necessary to get rid of attitudes, behaviors, and even ministries that are not producing either the fruit of the Spirit or Kingdom fruit. He writes, **"If we desire to become more generous ... we will have to make some practical decisions that cause us to leave some behaviors behind. To give more to God may mean reprioritizing and spending less on other things that do not lend life and build us up. We may have to prune some expenses and change some spending habits. . . ."** (p. 81) Similarly, he suggests that **"if we are doing work and offering ministries that are no longer shaping lives in significant ways, perhaps we should stop doing them."** (p. 81)

Week 4, Friday

Our generosity paves a way for those who follow us in the faith.

The author tells the story of a grandfather who changed his will to include the church after holding a child that wasn't his own after a baptism service one Sunday. It occurred to him later that the child *was* part of his family—part of his church family—and that he was grandfather to more than just his own. He realized he needed to provide for the children of the church as well as his own children and grandchildren. Schanse concludes, **"Those who practice Extravagant Generosity have a God-given vision and faith to plant seeds for trees whose shade they will never see."** (p. 84)

Week 4, Saturday

Fruitful congregations focus on giving throughout the year in a variety of ways and with all age groups.

The author dedicates this devotion to congregations that cultivate and practice Extravagant Generosity. He says that they...

- hold high-quality annual pledge opportunities with wide participation, excellent preparation, and active lay involvement.
- rely on the witness of extravagantly generous laypersons through testimonies, sermons, leadership talks, and newsletter/website reflections or devotions.
- recruit leaders who demonstrate personal growth in the practice of giving.
- emphasize generosity throughout the year in preaching, Bible studies, and classes.
- speak about the relationship between money and spiritual health.
- enter into major projects with excellence, professional preparation, and outstanding communication.
- offer members the opportunity to support special appeals and new projects.
- encourage charitable contributions and philanthropic giving by their members to groups and organizations outside the church.
- support special projects, missions in the community and around the world, and denominational connectional ministries.
- take the lead in responding to disasters and unexpected emergencies.
- develop mission partnerships and support agencies that help the poor.
- fund mission teams, scholarships, service projects, new church starts, and other ministries that transform lives.
- deepen the core ministries of worship, small group learning, and mission.
- teach, model, and cultivate generosity among children and youth.

Schnase writes, **"[Such churches] look for more and better opportunities to make a positive difference in the lives of people. . . . They make the mission of the church real, tangible, and meaningful. Their reputation for generosity bears witness to Christ." (p. 86)**

Week 4, Sunday

People who practice Extravagant Generosity give with joy, energy, and passion.

In this devotion, Schnase writes, **"*Extravagant* describes giving that is extraordinary, over-the-top, and propelled by great passion. *Extravagant* is the generosity seen in those who appreciate the beauty of giving, the awe and joy of making a difference for the purposes of Christ. Extravagant**

Generosity is giving to God as God has given to us." (p. 88) Such individuals give without fear and with greater trust.

Reflecting on the characteristics of those who give extravagantly, the author notes that they want to deepen their understanding of giving, grow in the grace of giving, make a difference for Jesus Christ, and teach or encourage others to be generous. He concludes, **"They like receiving money, find pleasure in its responsible use, and experience joy in giving it to God's purposes. They do not become too attached, and are not stopped, deceived, slowed, misled, or detoured in their following of Christ by the possession of money. They delight in Jesus' way, the way of true life." (p. 89)**

Group Discussion (15-20 minutes)
Select from the following:

1. Do you believe it is possible for us to love God without giving? Why or why not?
2. What does your current giving reveal about the condition of your heart? Of what you love?
3. What kind of person do you want to become over the next ten years? What kind of person do you believe God desires you to become? How are your current practices of living taking you there? How is your generosity helping you become who God wants you to be?
4. When do you first remember learning about giving? Who first modeled generosity for you?
5. How did you first learn about tithing? How does tithing shape the lives of people you know?
6. Do you tithe? If so, why? If not, why not? What causes you to resist growing in generosity?
7. How does living generously help you see the world through God's eyes?
8. How is your own philosophy of life shaped by the "wisdom of the world"—by materialism, consumerism, and the desire to possess? How is your philosophy of life shaped by the wisdom of God? How do you resolve the tensions between the two?
9. What attitudes, behaviors, and values might you need to prune in order to live more fruitfully in Christ?
10. How much planning, praying, and intentionality do you put into your decisions about giving? How would giving more generously require changes inside you and in your behaviors?
11. How have those who have come before you in your family, community, and church paved an easier road for you through their generosity?

How have you paved the road through your generosity for those who will follow you in the faith?

12. Would you describe your congregations as generous? Why or why not?

13. In what ways do you delight in the good you do through your giving?

14. Do you give more now than in the past, and do you expect to give more in the future than you do today? How are you learning to give more generously?

Group Activity (10-15 minutes)

Invite participants to respond briefly to the following questions. If you like, write their answers on a board or chart.

How have you stepped out of your comfort zone to express or declare your love for God through generous giving? What influenced you to do this?

Discuss how some of the ideas that have been shared encourage or inspire you to grow in your giving. Which of these practices, habits, or experiences would you like to try or adopt?

Based on this study, as well as your own experience, what are three or four things that are vitally important to generous giving?

Closing Prayer (2-5 minutes)

End with a time of prayer. You may use the prayer provided, offer your own prayer, invite someone from the group to pray (ask in advance, if possible), or allow participants to pray as they are led. If your group has a practice of sharing prayer concerns, do that first and pray for those requests as well.

> *God of abundant grace, you demonstrated Extravagant Generosity when you freely gave your Son. You call us to turn from our selfishness and self-centeredness and to embrace Christ, for it is only as we have in us the mind that was in Christ Jesus that we become free to be the compassionate, loving, and generous people you created us to be. Help us to overcome every challenge that would stand in our way—those that are external and those that are internal—so that we may continue growing in our love for you and in our desire to give. Make us passionate, enthusiastic, and extravagant givers who make a difference in the world for the sake of Christ. We pray that others will see the proof of our love for you and be changed—both by our example and by our actions. Amen.*

AFTER WEEK 4

A primary focus of the *Extravagant Generosity: The Heart of Giving* program is to reflect on and celebrate God's provision and, in response, to become a more generous people. In the first four weeks following the program, the pastor, program director, and leadership team will bring closure to the program through tasks such as

- Inviting response with Estimate of Giving Cards in worship

- Sending a follow-up mailing

- Reporting progress from the pulpit and other venues to celebrate and encourage giving

- Expressing appreciation through gift acknowledgments

- Using storytelling to celebrate God's work in the lives of members

In addition to these closure tasks, the church should pursue intentional efforts to retain and nurture new thoughts about giving and generosity on a year-round basis. Here are a few things that ongoing small groups can do to help keep the momentum going and encourage continued growth in generosity:

- Once a month, allow time for a few group members to share stories of how God is working in their lives, including how God is moving them toward greater generosity. Offer thanks together.

- Invite the pastor, program director, or someone from the leadership team to visit your group and share ongoing positive results with the class periodically.

- Plan several follow-up lessons/studies to conduct during the year. Choose some of the Scripture passages from Weeks 1-4 and explore these in more depth together. Or do a study on tithing, managing finances, or finding your spiritual gifts (many excellent group resources are available on these topics.)

- Six months after the program has ended, plan a group session in which you review the short videos from Weeks 1-4 and have a time for group discussion and sharing. What new insights do group members have now? What changes have they made in their lives as a result of the study?

- Coordinate several group projects throughout the year that will allow members to give generously of their time and service to others.

- Adopt a ministry, program, or cause to support financially as a group.

- Invite group members who are interested to form an Extravagant Generosity committee and brainstorm other ways the group can extend learning and application in the coming weeks and months.